To Tom & Marie
Our dear friends
With love
Chris and Maggi

BEYOND THE ENDLESS MOPANE

DEDICATION
To my parents, Doreen and Frank

A PHOTOGRAPHIC SAFARI THROUGH LIVINGSTONE'S AFRICA

BEYOND THE ENDLESS MOPANE

CHRIS HARVEY

CONTENTS

Introduction 9

1 Kalahari Sands and the Great Salt-pans 11

2 The Fresh Water and Lagoons of the Okavango Delta 37

3 The Wild Dogs of Moremi 49

4 The Linyanti and Savuti Marshes 81

5 The Chobe, Zambezi and Discovery of the Victoria Falls 121

Bibliography 144

First published in the UK in 1997
by Swan Hill Press, an imprint of Airlife Publishing Ltd

British Library Cataloguing in Publication Data
A catalogue record for this book
is available from the British Library

ISBN 1 85310 730 1

Typeset by Hewer Text Composition Services, Edinburgh
Printed in Singapore by Kyodo Printing Co. (S'pore) Pte Ltd

Swan Hill Press
an imprint of Airlife Publishing Ltd
101 Longden Road, Shrewsbury SY3 9EB

Buffalo (Syncerus caffer) travel great distances across the delta, always staying close to water and constantly on the move.

ACKNOWLEDGEMENTS

There are many people who have helped in different ways in the compilation of this book, and I would like to thank them all. The warmth and friendliness of the people I have met in Botswana during the years it took to compile the photographs contributed in no small way in encouraging me to complete the work.

First of all I would like to thank the office of the President for allowing me to photograph in Bostwana. I must thank Maggi Heinz for her undying support and assistance during this time while out in the bush.

I am indebted to John and Elaine Dugmore in Maun, for their terrific support and for providing a base for us there.

Also to Dougie and Diane Wright, of Ker and Downey, for their assistance and permission to photograph in their concession areas.

I wish to make a special acknowledgement to John and Tina Davey, while they were managing Mochaba Camp at Khwai, for giving me such great encouragement and help.

Thanks too to Karen Ross, an old friend at Conservation International, for her support, help and good advice.

Without the assistance and co-operation of Tico (John McNutt) and Lesley Boggs of the Botswana Wild Dog Research Project I would not have had such great opportunities with the wild dogs and to them I am especially grateful.

I would also like to mention Lionel Palmer for his own brand of advice and humour, and Jeff Baum.

Peter Perlstein of Wildlife Helicopters in Maun. His skill in helping me with the aerial work made a significant contribution to the book.

Thanks to Graeme Labe of Gametrackers (Maun) for permitting me to photograph in their concession areas and to Brian and Val Bartlett at Linyanti for their hospitality. Also the Honourable Mr Justice Barrington Jones in Lobatse and Lisa Hansen in Namibia.

In South Africa I would like to express my appreciation to Dorothy Fluke, Graham Williams, Lloyd and Sheila Williams, Myra Williams, Bernard and Paula Price, Michael and Francis Slabber, John Baxter and James Bissett who have helped enormously during our stays in Cape Town.

In Johannesburg I owe a special thanks to Mike, Rob and Hilary Crawford for helping us out there.

In England I am indebted to Michael Shaw, my agent at Curtis Brown, and to Alastair Simpson of the Swan Hill Press without whose support this book would not have happened.

Also special thanks to Heidi Cameron of the World Wide Fund for Nature (UK) and to Robert Farrar and Bernie Vent of Alchemy in London for their excellent work.

A final thanks to all my friends and family who have encouraged me along the way.

A cheetah at full speed can reach 110 kph.

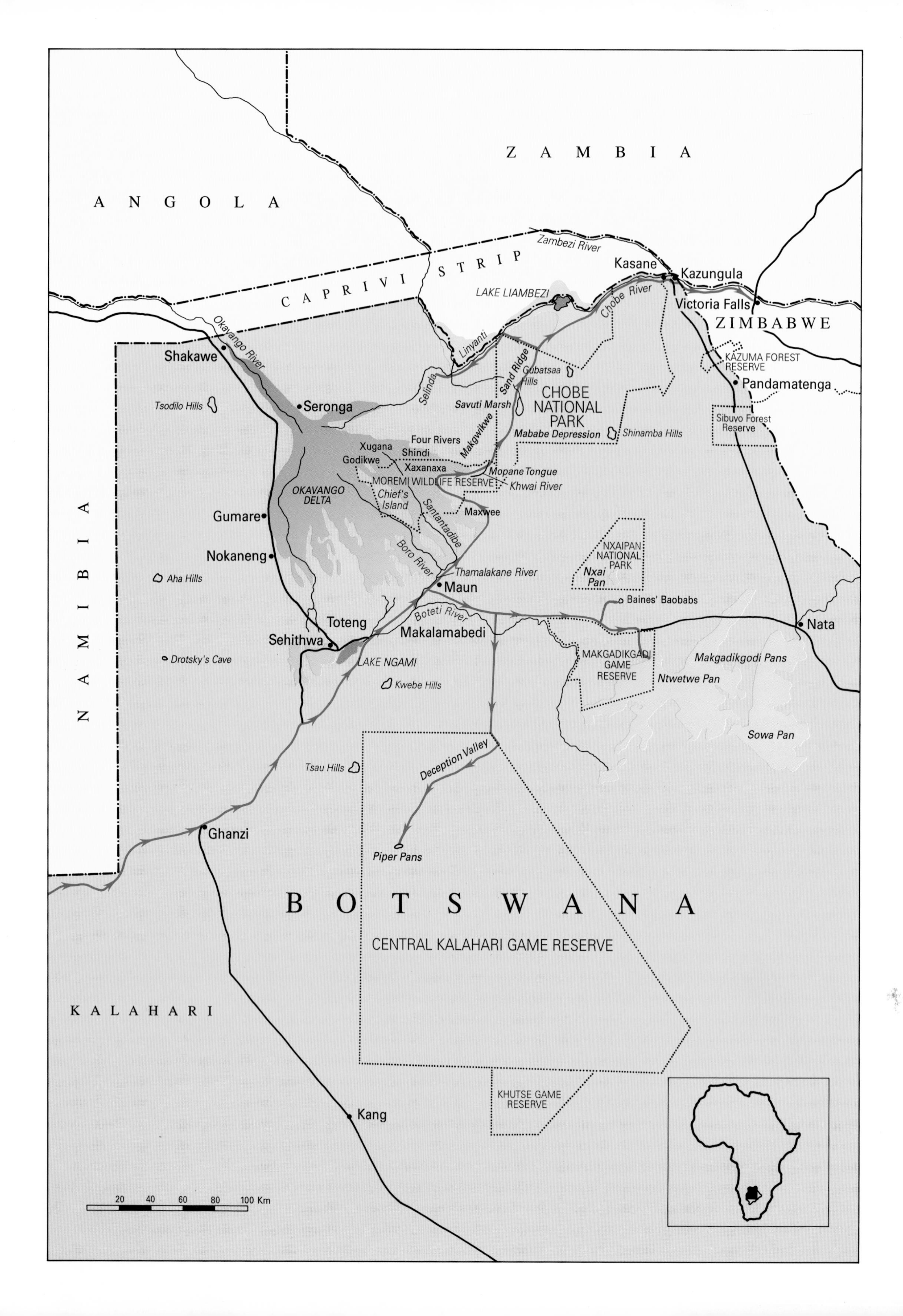
ZAMBIA
ANGOLA
Zambezi River
CAPRIVI STRIP
Kasane
Kazungula
LAKE LIAMBEZI
Chobe River
Victoria Falls
ZIMBABWE
Okavango River
Shakawe
Linyanti
Sand Ridge
Gubatsaa Hills
KAZUMA FOREST RESERVE
Selinda
Pandamatenga
Tsodilo Hills
Seronga
Savuti Marsh
CHOBE NATIONAL PARK
Makgwikwe
Sibuyo Forest Reserve
Four Rivers
Mababe Depression
Shinamba Hills
Xugana
Shindi
Godikwe
Xaxanaxa
Mopane Tongue
MOREMI WILDLIFE RESERVE
Khwai River
OKAVANGO DELTA
Chief's Island
Santantadibe
Maxwee
Gumare
NAMIBIA
NXAIPAN NATIONAL PARK
Nxai Pan
Boro River
Nokaneng
Thamalakane River
Aha Hills
Maun
Baines' Baobabs
Boteti River
Toteng
Nata
Makalamabedi
Sehithwa
MAKGADIKGADI GAME RESERVE
Makgadikgodi Pans
Drotsky's Cave
LAKE NGAMI
Ntwetwe Pan
Kwebe Hills
Sowa Pan
Deception Valley
Tsau Hills
Ghanzi
Piper Pans
BOTSWANA
CENTRAL KALAHARI GAME RESERVE
KALAHARI
KHUTSE GAME RESERVE
Kang
20 40 60 80 100 Km

INTRODUCTION

'There is a fascination to me in the remembrance of the free life, the self dependence, the feeling as you lay under your caross that you were looking at the stars from a point on earth whence no other European had ever seen them; the hope that every patch of bush was the only thing between you and some strange scene – these are with me still. Were I not married with grandchildren I should head back to Africa and end my days in the open air. It is useless to tell me of civilization. Take the word of one who has tried both, there is a charm in the wild life.'

WILLIAM COTTON OSWELL, 1893

Across Botswana's vast, flat landscape, Kalahari sands cover almost the entire country. As you travel north, the dry thirstland of sand dunes, thorn scrub, pans and grasslands gives way to woodlands, which stretch for miles in a broad belt across the northern part of Botswana. Acacia and combretum are common, but the dominant species is the mopane tree.

David Livingstone remarked on how little shade the tree afforded. This is because its butterfly-shaped leaves close up during the heat of the day. In summer these woodlands are a canopy of green, but in winter the leaves turn red and fall. For a few weeks the woodlands are bare, offering little shade from the oppressive heat. Trees stand like grey statues on a rust-coloured carpet. From the air it looks a forbidding place. Few animals other than wandering elephants can live here at this time, for all life centres around the floodplains where the rivers are at their fullest, due to the arrival of floodwaters from the Okavango. These rivers are lifelines for the wildlife – beyond, the bare woodlands stretch endlessly over the horizon until the army of trees is finally halted by a great barrier of fresh waterways and lagoons, palms and papyrus. The Okavango Delta, Linyanti and Chobe rivers are home to great concentrations of animals. A wetland paradise that has been the destination of many explorers and travellers. Beyond the endless mopane.

Livingstone, Oswell, Chapman, Baines and other great explorers became legends here. Romantic tales of their exploits and discoveries in Darkest Africa enthralled the Victorian public in England. Few people had even seen a picture of an elephant or lion and the belief in the savagery of Wild Africa added to the sense of danger and adventure.

These men did take considerable risks, but disease and fever were their worst enemies. Their journeys took many months, which added to the remoteness of these places. Today you could be flown out and be in hospital the same day. Still, names like Linyanti, Savuti, Chobe and the Kalahari do have a magical ring to them and every traveller is filled with expectancy and excitement at the thought of what he might experience there.

Since my first visit to Botswana in 1981, it has changed little. But access to this great wilderness area is becoming easier, with the old sandy tracks being replaced by graded or tarred roads. More people can afford four-wheel-drive vehicles today and it is this influx of people that is going to force change.

Donkey power for a bushman family near Ghanzi.

I decided to go back to Botswana with my girlfriend Maggi, and, with no pressures or time limits, experience the Africa of Livingstone and Chapman with its wonderful animals. Entering Botswana from Gobabis in Namibia we would follow the old road to Ghanzi and on to Maun, then travel east to the great salt-pans of the Makgadikgadi through which Livingstone trekked on his way to the Chobe. From the pans the journey would take us north-west to the Okavango Delta, Moremi, Linyanti and the Chobe. Our destination would be the Victoria Falls in Zimbabwe.

This book is my tribute to the animals of Botswana. Long may they continue to survive and give the same experiences and pleasures to others as they have given to me.

Chapter One
Kalahari Sands and the Great Salt-Pans

(Acacia Erioloba) – Mogotlo – camelthorn

The journey from Cape Town was an easy drive on good tarred roads until we reached the quiet frontier post at Mowane on the Namibia–Botswana border. It took just two and a half days of travel through changing country. From the orchards and vineyards of Citrusdal in South Africa, across the Orange River into Namibia, where the long, straight, tarred road cuts between the western edge of the Kalahari and the Namib Deserts.

On reaching the capital, Windhoek, we turned due east and within three hours had left the luxury of the tarred road to cross into Botswana. The border officials were polite and friendly and it felt good to be back. Immediately the quality of the road deteriorated and for the next few hours we literally crashed along the broken calcrete surface towards the cattle centre in the Kalahari, Ghanzi. Severe corrugation in places shattered the nerves and everything in the Toyota Hilux bounced around in a crazy fashion.

After a couple of hours of this I pulled over and stopped under the shade of a camelthorn tree. My eyeballs were still bouncing around as I stepped out of the cab. It was April, but unusually hot. The sand was burning through the soles of my boots. Maggi opened the back of the Hilux and looked in despair as she tried to locate the Thermos flask and coffee. The neatly packed system had been totally rearranged.

I was aware of a calm silence as the hum of the engine no longer filled my ears. Just the sound of the wind. I noticed a kudu standing under a camelthorn a few hundred metres away. A majestic dark silhouette with spiral horns set against the glaring light beyond. The blond grass waved gently in the breeze. Apart from the fences everywhere, little had changed since James Chapman and Thomas Baines travelled this road over one hundred years ago with their wagons, horses and oxen.

When I glanced up again at the camelthorn tree, the kudu had vanished.

Back on the road I was abruptly separated from the silence as we bounced onward on the seemingly endless road. As we neared Ghanzi, more traffic appeared in the form of an old truck, a couple of brand new Toyota Landcruisers, some guys on horses obligingly herding their cattle off the road for us, and a Bushman and his family going to town in a cart hauled by a team of donkeys. The cart must have been his pride and joy, for it had rubber-tyred wheels and rear lights with indicators, crudely wired up to what I assumed was a battery in the front. I doubt whether they worked! The passengers all looked quite serious till we smiled and waved as we passed. They all responded with broad grins and waved back. I couldn't resist taking a picture and the twenty pula I offered made them grin even more!

This is excellent cattle country. It was this that attracted settlers to trek across the Kalahari in 1895, lured by false promises.

During this period the European powers were colonizing the African continent. Botswana, then Bechuanaland, was administered by Britain. Namibia was then German South-West Africa, and the Germans had ambitions to settle in this desolate region. Cecil Rhodes was anxious to protect his British South Africa Company and he persuaded the authorities to encourage farmers to develop the region and deter German ideas of expansion. Within a few years, with promises of cheap drilling equipment to sink boreholes, the first settlers made the journey that became known as the Rhodes Trek. However, the people were not experienced farmers, many of them merely trying to escape from the poor conditions they suffered in the Transvaal. A rather dubious beginning, but the town did eventually prosper and many living there today are descended from those original settlers.

Some years earlier, in 1875, a Dutchman called Hendrik van Zyl first visited Ghanzi and began work on an extravagant home which he furnished in expensive European style. He must have been a very wealthy man and wielded tremendous power and influence as a land baron until his mysterious death in 1880. There were substantial numbers of elephants in the area at that time and it is said van Zyl killed over one hundred in one day at a place called Olifants Pan. He sent the ivory to Cape Town and made huge profits.

The years after the Rhodes Trek were bad for Ghanzi, and by the time the Boer War broke out in 1899 few farms could be said to be going concerns. The war, though, encouraged a general movement around southern Africa and afterwards cattle speculating became good business.

The town today is the administrative centre of Ghanzi District. It stands on a calcrete ridge that stretches all the way to Windhoek, some 500 km away. A water table lies beneath the shallow sands.

The Kalahari nights can be cold, sometimes freezing in July. The morning we left Ghanzi it was only 8°C. Dewdrops on the tips of the grass caught the early rays of the sun and shone like little stars. The Hilux, which we call 'Egret', felt quite damp as the motor reluctantly spluttered into life and we set off towards Maun.

As we neared Maun, the road took us close to Lake Ngami. You can't see the lake from the road and it takes a bit of guesswork to find a track that will lead you to it. Nowadays the lake is dry and unrecognisable as trees have grown on parts of the lakebed. However, in 1848 it was of great significance.

In those days people had heard of a great lake to the north of the Kalahari. Nobody had succeeded in finding it and many doubted its existence. It was generally thought that the Kalahari was a great desert like the Sahara in North Africa. William Cotton Oswell and his friend Mungo Murray decided to finance an expedition to find Lake Ngami (the name means 'great water') and prove that it was possible to cross the Kalahari. In 1845 Oswell had met Livingstone at Mabotse and he had expressed a great desire to explore the region, believing there was well-watered land to the north where there would be many native tribes 'waiting for Christianity'.

Oswell and Murray invited Livingstone to join them and in 1849 the men set off. Oswell generously gave Livingstone, who had little money of his own, a wagon and oxen. Oswell wrote of the extreme difficulty experienced in crossing the soft sand over which the horses and oxen laboured. A baKwain from the

Lake Ngami, discovered by Oswell, Murray and Livingstone.

From a drawing made on the spot (1550) by the late Alfred Ryder, Esq.

Boteti River guided the expedition and they finally reached the river, which was then called the Zouga, after nearly running out of water. Following the Boteti west for 450 km, they finally stood on the shores of the lake, then full of water. Oswell wrote, 'None save those who have suffered from the want, know the beauty of water. A magnificent sheet without bound gladdened our eyes.' Oswell's account was read to the Royal Geographical Society in London in 1850, but Livingstone had already stolen the limelight, claiming the discovery for himself. Nobody actually cared who had organized the expedition.

The chief of the baTawana was Letsholathebe, son of Chief Moremi, and he spoke of great river systems to the north, confirming what Livingstone already suspected. This inspired the doctor to continue northward, but Letsholathebe refused to provide boats to cross the Boteti, then a great river. The plan had to be shelved and it was not until their third expedition, two years later, that Oswell and Livingstone went beyond the Boteti by way of the Makgadikgadi Pans and finally reached the Chobe in 1850.

James Chapman and Thomas Baines also visited Ngami a few years later. Letsholathebe persuaded the explorers to stay, and Chapman attempted to photograph the chief and his entourage. However, as soon as Chapman put the black cloth over his head and camera, the natives took fright and fled!

As we stared across the dry lake, I tried to imagine the fishing boats, the pelicans and hippos. There is one interesting theory as to why the lake is often dry. . . . When guns became available to the baTawana they began to kill the hippos which constantly raided their crops. Each year as the hippo population dwindled, the Nhabe River, which flowed into Lake Ngami, became more choked with reeds. Eventually they blocked the channels which the hippos used to keep open. Then the river burst its ancient banks and that much water never found its way into Lake Ngami again.

Maun is the safari centre of the Okavango and is situated on the Thamalakane River, which joins the Boteti just north of Lake Ngami. As we drove through the outskirts of the town everything seemed much the same as when we had last been there, three years before. There were still plenty of the traditional thatched rondavels, but new square huts, with tin roofs, were springing up everywhere. The centre of Maun had changed a lot. There were new shopping complexes, street lamps, a pedestrian crossing and a roundabout on the main high street. The old Rileys garage had gone, making way for a new building adjoining a row of shops and boutiques around the parking area. It was obvious that business was booming in the tourist industry, on which Maun depends.

We passed the airfield, where dozens of light aircraft were parked in neat rows, awaiting their next missions to the many camps in the delta.

We decided to drive down the road to Kalahari Kanvas, a tent-manufacturing business run by Elaine Dugmore. As always there was a warm welcome and we talked about the changing face of Maun. Elaine's husband John walked in, accompanied by Lionel Palmer. Both men were professional hunters for many years and know the delta intimately. I felt a surge of unease as they talked about the diminishing numbers of wildlife. Nobody could seem to put their finger on why, but buffalo and zebra were declining rapidly. There seemed to be several reasons, perhaps all contributing: the recent drought, the fences and, most likely of all, hunting and the misuse of citizen's licences. Lionel suggested we go over to Peter Perlstein at Wildlife Helicopters. 'He's flying all the time and knows what's about. Get him to take you over the Santantadibe. There's usually a lot of buffalo around there.'

Smoking dagga is a favourite pastime.

The Central Kalahari Game Reserve was set up as much for the bushmen as for the wildlife. Since the sinking of boreholes, however, settlements have been established around these permanent water supplies and the old ways are disappearing.

Fossil riverbeds wind their way through the dunes across the Kalahari.

Kalahari sands cover much of Southern Africa but the Kalahari itself is rich in flora and fauna, the sand ridges and dunes being stabilised by grasses and drought-resistant trees. In the northern part of the Kalahari lie the great salt-pans of Makgadikgadi, legacy of a great super lake.

John and Elaine invited us to stay that night, but first we took their advice and went over to see Peter.

Peter Perlstein is a friendly chap and always enthusiastic about any area you may wish to visit. 'There's a big herd of buffalo near the Moremi at the moment, just west of the Santantadibe River. I reckon there's well over a thousand. It's so dry at the moment you can drive right in there.' The area he was talking about is outside the game reserve, but animals wander in and out of the reserves freely. There are no fences, except the long cordon fence that runs west of Maun up to the Gomoti River where it turns north-east just south of Moremi. To the east of the fence the land is for cattle, to the west and north is wilderness.

Peter suggested we went up early the next morning. Excitedly Maggi and I agreed, although we had intended to head east to the Makgadikadi. The prospect of photographing hundreds of buffalo won the day and after a comfortable night with the Dugmores we turned up just after sunrise at the airfield. The helicopter was refuelled and the doors taken off. Within minutes we were up and away, ascending into a crisp, blue autumn sky.

Below us the land was dry. Maun had had very little rain this year. The thatched huts were soon left behind as we swung out over the buffalo cordon fence. We had only been airborne for ten minutes when Peter's voice came over the headset. 'You see that dust over on the horizon? That's the buffalo.' It looked like smoke from a fire, but as the helicopter swooped closer we could make out hundreds of black shapes in long columns. Peter made a low pass and the buffalo swung away in a huge, rolling mass. They broke into a canter, raising even more dust. It was really an amazing sight. Leaning out of the helicopter my fishing jacket flapped like a flag in a gale-force wind. Roll after roll of film was eaten up by the motor-driven camera. Close-ups, wide angles, the picture opportunities were endless. After making one more pass we decided not to harass the animals any longer. I knew I had got some good shots.

As we flew back to Maun, I realized the importance of getting pictures from the air. Everything looked so much more explicit and the lie of the land was easier to understand. This was to be the first of a number of trips we made with Peter.

After stocking up with food and petrol we took the new tarred road out of Maun towards Nata. That night we would camp out on a pan beside some huge baobabs, under a nearly full moon.

Pronking springbok (Antidorcas marsupialis) show off their agility when threatened. After good rains the fresh grass on the pans attracts them in thousands.

I remember the old gravel road to Nata well. It was an adventure in itself to drive along, being constantly enveloped in a cloud of fine white dust from passing vehicles. Now it was easy, save for the cattle and donkeys which regularly stray across the new tarred road. As we approached the Nxai Pan turn-off, I noticed a number of dead animals lying by the roadside, including a bat-eared fox. A donkey, probably killed by a vehicle, had been picked clean by vultures which stood motionless close by. At night the roads are a death zone for animals that get dazzled by the headlights of speeding vehicles.

The turn-off to Nxai Pan is a soft, sandy track. We drove for about 30 km and turned right at a small sign towards Baines' Baobabs. About 5 km after the sign the road forks. Both tracks lead to the baobabs, but we decided to take the left one as recent heavy rain in the area would almost certainly have made the pans, over which you must cross, very treacherous.

Keeping to the most well-used tracks, we drove across a large plain. Gemsbok were feeding in the distance. Then we spotted the seven baobabs, very obvious as there are few large trees around. They are named after the artist Thomas Baines, who painted them in 1862. The trees stand on the northern edge of Kudiakam Pan, one of the most northerly salt-pans in the Makgadikgadi. The recent rain had half-filled Kudiakam Pan. In the distance we spotted a group of pelicans standing motionless. Apart from the occasional call of a black korhaan, it is only the wind that breaks the silence. The dry soda on the edge of the pan, not covered with water, reflected warmth on to our skins, contrasting with the coolness of the wind. As the sun went down, turning the whiteness of the pan to changing hues of blue and pink, the moon was already rising behind us. It was nearly full and, as the sky darkened, its brilliance took over, illuminating the pan. A dark shape darted out of the grass and stopped a few paces from us. A jackal setting out on its nocturnal wanderings.

We had parked on the edge of the pan. In a few minutes we had set up the roof tent on the Hilux and heated up a bowl of soup. It was time to reflect on the experiences of the day. Tired, we climbed up the ladder into the tent. The eerie cry of the jackals drifted across the pan.

The vast salt-pans of Ntwetwe and Sua, collectively known as the Makgadikgadi Pans, lie in the centre of Botswana on the northern edge of the Kalahari and are the largest salt-pans in the world. On the southern side of the pans lies a steep, prehistoric shoreline, indicating that there was once a great lake here, fed by rivers that have long since dried up or changed their course. To the west of Ntwetwe Pan, the great rolling plains of the Makgadikgadi Game Reserve are home to large herds of zebra during the early winter months. Stretching across the northern edge of the plains a wide belt of hyphaene palms grow. It is thought that elephants once roamed here and dispersed the seeds of their fruit. Favouring a shallow, saline water table, they are the only trees that thrive on these grasslands that were once the bed of the great lake.

On the northern shore of Ntwetwe, just south of Gweta, stands a huge baobab on which you can find the initials of Thomas Baines. The baobab has been named after James Chapman, who led that expedition. It had taken Chapman and Baines six hours to cross Ntwetwe Pan from the south-east. On 10 July 1862, he described his impressions of the great salt-pan:

> The lake is like a vast white and calm sea. In the centre we could not see the banks on either side. A cold wind conveyed with it a white saltish substance into the eyes of dogs, horses, men and cattle. All of which showed symptoms of the pain they were enduring. . . . Had a large fire made and some delicious giraffe steak and coffee. Left this and passed a large Mowana tree, the circumference at the base is 29 yards. It is now leafless and looks like a castle.

Seas of grass (Chloris virgata) grow amongst the dunes in the Kalahari. In the autumn the grass heads seed, displaying many varieties.

Livingstone and Oswell had passed the baobab twelve years earlier. Livingstone described the tree best in his book *Missionary Travels*:

> We passed over the immense pan Ntwetwe on which the latitude could be taken as at sea . . . about two miles beyond the northern bank of the pan we unyoked under a fine specimen of the baobab, here called in the language of the Bechuanas, Mowana; it consisted of six branches united into one trunk. At three feet from the ground it was eighty five feet in circumference.

Interestingly there is only a discrepancy of about 2 feet (60 cm) in the measurements of Chapman and Livingstone. Standing under the same tree now, 145 years later, we too were struck by its size and composition. Since Baines left his initials on its trunk, many people have added to them. Livingstone inscribed only one tree in all his travels, on an island on the Zambezi overlooking the Victoria Falls. He excused it as 'the only instance in which I indulged in this piece of vanity'.

The great herds of wildebeest have sadly diminished on the Makadikgadi and, although these animals can still be found on the plains, their migrations, which could once rival those of the Serengeti, are a mere shadow of their former splendour.

As we drove closer to the pans, the going became heavier. The recent rain had turned it into thick, sticky mud, made worse in places where vehicles had bogged down, leaving deep ruts in the track. Our search for the zebra herds was not going well. I could sense Maggi's apprehension as we ground our way through the patches of deep mud in low-ratio four-wheel drive. The fuel gauge was dropping alarmingly and in one hour we covered only 8 km!

'What if we get stuck out here?' she asked. The thought had crossed my mind as well and the worse the track got the tenser we both became. I decided to stop. All around us the sea of grass extended to every horizon, broken only by the odd cluster of palms. We had not seen much all morning except for a few ostrich and gemsbok. Maggie clambered up on the roof with the binoculars to scan the horizon.

'There they are!' she shouted excitedly. 'There must be hundreds of them.'

I hoisted myself up top and focused on countless striped images shimmering in the heat rising from the ground. To the south there were long columns of zebra walking lazily across the plains, some nodding their heads as they went. The procession seemed endless.

The problem facing us now was, having found the zebra, how were we to get close? Not only was the track treacherous, but it was heading away from the direction we wanted to go. The zebra must have been a couple of kilometres away and I knew that if we tried to approach they would only run. Out on the open plains animals are naturally suspicious of anything making a bee-line for them. I also wondered what traps lay out there for us. We could easily have got stuck in the mud and there were no trees to which we could attach the winch.

Photography can be a very frustrating activity, and I accepted the fact that the only way we were going to get good shots would be with the help of Peter's helicopter. It would also give a much better impression of Ntwetwe, which we couldn't get near to anyway. We decided to turn back to Maun.

Once we were back on the tarred road we made good progress. As we passed the Makalamabedi turn-off thoughts of the Kalahari flashed through my mind. We still had 200 litres of fuel and plenty of food with us. Although the Makgadikgadi had defeated us for the time being, the lure of the Kalahari was too great to resist. 'Let's go to Deception,' I said, pulling to the side of the road. Maggi's face beamed and with renewed enthusiasm we took the road to Makalamabedi.

Deception Valley is a long, ancient river course in the north of the Central

Kalahari Game Reserve. There are a series of pans along the valley, so called because of the sand ridges that run along each side. In April, large herds of springbok and gemsbok can be found there, but its main attraction lies in its remoteness.

The road to Makalamabedi is tarred now, as far as the Boteti River. However, on reaching the bridge we were disappointed to find it bone dry; when I crossed here several years earlier, it had been flowing. Now donkeys and cattle grazed on the riverbed as if it were a huge meadow. The great river that Livingstone wrote about was history.

He described a new species of antelope, the lechwe, and how 'along the beautifully wooded river we came to a large stream flowing into it. This was the river Tamunakle [Thamalakane] and I enquired whence it came.'

It was here that Livingstone learned of the great rivers to the north:

> The prospect of a highway capable of being traversed by boats to an entirely unexplored and very populous region grew from that time stronger and stronger in my mind. So much so that when we came to the lake [Ngami] this idea occupied such a large portion of my mental vision that the actual discovery seemed of little importance.

A full moon rises in the twilight of the setting sun.

So it was that, on the Boteti, Livingstone turned from missionary to explorer.

Once across the bridge a dirt road took over as far as the small town of Makalamabedi, which is situated next to a cut-line fence that separates wildlife from cattle and reaches 80 km due south into the Kalahari, where it meets the Kuke fence at right angles. This is the northern boundary of the Central Kalahari Game Reserve.

It took about an hour and a half to reach Kuke Corner, where a smiling Bushman, wearing an official cap, noted our registration number and let us pass through the gate. We were leaving cattle country and headed south-east along another fence which ended abruptly after just 15 km, as if someone had forgotten to finish it. At this point there is a crossroad and a sign pointing east to Rakops. The track to the west had a large sign beside it telling us that we were entering the Central Kalahari Game Reserve. However, it was getting late and we were tired from the long journey. Pulling off the track, we set up the roof tent amongst some low acacias. The next day we would be in Deception Valley.

After an early start we soon came to the game scouts' camp where we topped up our water containers. There would be no water from here on and we would be able to stay only as long as our four 20-litre containers lasted. I reckoned our petrol would easily outlast the water.

Leaving the game scouts' camp behind we drove through typical duneland before descending on to a pan studded with low camelthorn trees. The Kalahari is not a true desert. It is not short of vegetation and there are plenty of trees. It is the undependable rains and lack of surface water, for most of the time, that puts it into the category of a desert.

After about 30 km we drove over the crest of a sand ridge; stretching out before us lay Deception Valley.

Six years had gone by since my last visit and most of that trip was spent stuck on a muddy pan. A few more people come down here now since the Central Kalahari has been opened to the public, but it is not a good place to be stranded.

This time I wanted to get a lot further along the valley. The track down the sand ridge descended gradually on to the valley floor, where there were many springbok. Grazing close to the track, they did not even look up as we drove past.

The nocturnal brown hyena (Hyaena brunnea) is still active on cold winter mornings.

Deception Pan itself may have got its name from the grey clay it contains; being an oval shape, from the air it looks quite like a water-filled lake. Deception Valley, like other ancient river courses, winds its way into the Kalahari and just fades away.

As we drove along the valley we were captivated by a feeling of freedom and space. The wide valley floor stretched ahead of us, inviting us to continue. Gently sloping dunes, held firm by blond grasses and acacia trees, rose on either side. In what seemed an inhospitable environment, life thrived. Springbok, gemsbok and wildebeest grazed on the pans. Ground squirrels charged energetically around while groups of suricates dug frantically in the sand.

Our second day in Deception was hot and in places the flies drove us mad when we tried to relax during the middle of the day. The further along the valley we drove, the smaller and smaller the trees seemed to get, offering little shade. In the afternoons strong winds blew up the dust, forcing us to take refuge in the Hilux. We were totally dependent on 'Egret'. She was our mobile home. The roof tent proved its worth time and again. At night we would pull out a couple of chairs and a table and cook on a gas ring. The desert was our dining room and we ate under a full moon to the sound of dozens of barking geckos.

We had travelled over 100 km and the wide valley floor of Deception began to fade away. The track took us over dunes and back down on to small pans. Eventually we came over the crest of another dune and to the side of the road there was a little sign. We had arrived at Piper Pans. The track wound its way down on to a large pan covered in yellow grass.

On the opposite side of the pan, in the distance, a tree line ran along the foot of the dunes. It was getting hot by this time and we decided to head for these trees and relax for the afternoon in the shade.

We drove down on to the pan past grazing herds of springbok and gemsbok. The nearer we got to the trees the smaller they became. When we reached them we could not even park 'Egret' under their shade. In fact there were no tall trees anywhere!

We were deep in the central Kalahari and yet there was still this lure to see over the next horizon. Piper Pans are a series of three large pans. On the second there is a permanent waterhole fed from a pump. It must have been the only water for miles, but it did not look very inviting. We still had over 40 litres of clear borehole water, half of what we had set out with. This was going to be the furthest we would go.

We noticed a tall tree just off the track leading to the third pan. As we approached I spotted a dark mound beneath it.

'It's a lion,' Maggi exclaimed.

Unbelievably the only reasonable tree we could have used was already occupied by a large, black-maned lion. He really was in superb condition. We had to smile and, not wishing to disturb him, decided to leave him alone for now. We would return later in the afternoon. It took us an hour to find another tree!

As the sun sank behind the dunes, the sky glowed a brilliant orange. The moon was not up yet. I was hoping to get a shot of the lion against the sunset, but he was still lying under the tree, not concerned with us. As the last hues of red faded away, darkness descended quickly. A cue for the lion to roar. It seemed only a gesture really, like something he felt obliged to do, for he never raised his head during the whole performance. He just lay where he was and roared. A few moments later he did lift his head, then sat up and yawned. Laboriously rising to his feet, he walked a few paces out on to the pan and sat down again, gazing into the fading twilight.

I drove quietly closer, getting clear of the tree and surrounding bushes. Behind the lion a red glow began ascending like a great red ball. I hurriedly put my flash together with a camera, quietly eased myself out of the cab and slid under the Hilux. At ground level the moon was right behind the lion's head. Maggi switched on the spotlight so that I could focus. In seconds the moon had turned to a fiery orange, like a great golden orb. The lion looked perfect.

'That's it,' I thought as I pressed the shutter. Nothing. The camera was empty. How stupid! I had forgotten to reload. I slid backwards, eased myself up into the cab and scrabbled in the back to get a new roll of film.

'He's moving,' Maggi whispered.

I cursed myself. It would have been a great shot. The opportunity had gone.

We followed the lion for an hour back out on to the first pan, then lost him as he went up into the dunes. He had offered me a superb opportunity and I had messed it up.

As we lay in the roof tent that night, I thought of where we were. Alone and miles from anyone. It was a humbling thought, but to experience this kind of solitude was a privilege. I had no love for urban life and out here there was no stress. Nature was making no demands, we were here only as observers, passing through. As I drifted into slumber, the lion roared in the dunes.

Leaving Deception a few days later was not easy. It is a special place and we vowed that one day we would return.

A couple of days later we were back at Ntwetwe, in Peter's helicopter. Rainwater had partially filled the pan and it resembled a vast estuary. In a month or so these ephemeral waters would be gone, sucked up by the clay and then baked dry by the sun. We found the zebra herds and felt once again that it was only from the air that the vastness of these plains could really be appreciated.

The most common mammal is the ground squirrel (Xerus inauris). Large numbers live on the pans and fossil riverbeds where the harder sand enables them to dig elaborate burrows. They use their bushy tails as a sunshade while foraging in the heat.

A suricate (Suricata suricatta) digs for insects. Although not as common as the ground squirrel, they will occupy squirrel burrows, or excavate their own. Moving around their territories, sentries are constantly alert for birds of prey or jackals and give frequent 'all-clear' calls to the foragers in the form of high pitched chirps.

The suricates are only active in daylight and sleep in a burrow at night, coming out to warm themselves at sunrise. They eat arthropods and immobilise scorpions by first biting off their sting. To avoid overuse of an area within their territory the group move from one burrow to another.

The long orange legs of the pale chanting goshawk (Melierax poliopterus) are distinctive. It is a resident of semi-desert bush areas and is common in the Kalahari. It eats rodents, lizards, termites and scorpions as well as the eggs and young of small birds. The goshawk can often be seen in the company of honey badgers, waiting for scraps.

Although mainly nocturnal, the African wildcat (Felis lybica) can often be seen at twilight. They are common in varied habitats and are the size of a domestic cat. It is believed that the ancient Egyptians first domesticated them and today's domestic cats are their descendants.

Honey badgers (Mellivora capensis) can often be seen foraging late into the morning during winter. They feed on reptiles, insects and scorpions and of course honey. It is completely fearless and very aggressive. Even lions will avoid it.

Gemsbok cows (Oryx gazella) sparring, probably for status within the herd. Territorial disputes between dominant bulls can end in death. The long rapier-like horns can be used for stabbing an opponent and are a lethal weapon. Lions can suffer serious injury, or death, when tackling one of these antelopes. Gemsbok are adapted to desert conditions and are not dependent on water. They rely on wild melons and cucumbers and will also feed during the night when cool temperatures increase the water content of vegetation.

ABOVE: *Sudden and violent rainstorms sweep the Kalahari in October and November. Within weeks the desert is transformed.*

A pygmy falcon (Poliohierax semitorquatus) bathes in rainwater collected in a deep tyre track. The little raptor will often nest in social weaver nests.

OPPOSITE: *Cheetahs (Acinonyx jubata) will take many springbok during the lambing season. The pans of the Kalahari can be excellent places to watch cheetah hunting.*

Hungry young cheetah cubs watch intently as their mother returns with a kill. They will sometimes eat twice a day during the springbok lambing season.

Blue wildebeest (Connochaetas tarinus) numbers crashed in the Kalahari after fences blocked all their migration routes. A couple of the ungulates kick up fine dust in the light of the setting sun.

OPPOSITE: *Like most cats the serval (Felis serval) is nocturnal and solitary. Its large ears can locate rodents in long grass over which it will leap to catch prey. Here a serval comically bites a piece of bristle grass, locally called mouse's tail, which is very appropriate for this caption.*

A sandy track winds down a dune onto Piper Pans, deep in the central Kalahari. It is early April and after good summer rains, the sand dunes are covered in lush green vegetation.

Chapman's Baobab, named after the photographer-explorer James Chapman, stands on the northern edge of Ntwetwe Pan, south of Gweta. This huge tree measures 26.5 metres in circumference, at the base. David Livingstone also mentions this tree in his book Missionary Travels*, he camped here on his expedition to the Chobe in 1851.*

RIGHT, TOP: *Baines' Baobabs, named after the artist Thomas Baines, overlook a water-filled Kudiakam Pan. These ancient trees dominate the surrounding flat landscape.*

RIGHT, BOTTOM: *Rain-filled Ntwetwe Pan stretches way beyond the horizon behind a group of Hypheane palm trees, a common feature in the Makgadikgadi.*

OPPOSITE: *After late summer rains Ntwetwe Pan resembles a vast estuary. Joined to Sua Pan in the east, the Makgadikgadi Pans measure over 100 km from east to west.*

The rich grasslands of the plains, bordering the pans to the west, attract large herds of zebra in the late summer months.

The zebra herds travel huge distances in their search for fresh grazing.

CHAPTER TWO
THE FRESH WATER AND LAGOONS OF THE OKAVANGO DELTA

(Hyphaene Petersiana) – *Mokolwane* – *Real Fan Palm*

The Okavango is geographically part of the Kalahari. It is like a great river that has got lost while looking for the sea. Formed on Kalahari sand when the great lake of Makgadikgadi dried up over 20 million years ago, and with nowhere to go, the river spread out looking for drainage. Today it is the largest inland delta in the world. However, if the delta dried up, the true Kalahari would reclaim this paradise. Maybe one day it will happen and people will say, 'There were once lechwe and hippo here. . . .'

The river system of the delta is very complex. In fact the rivers are really drainage channels. If you compared the delta to the root system of a tree, then the Okavango would be the main trunk. This is the panhandle and beyond this point you are at the base of the tree where the roots fan out. The channels on the extremities are the Taoghe River, running south, and the Selinda Spillway, running north-east. In the centre you have the Boro, Xudum and the Nqugha river channels. The Nqugha forms its own little delta as it forks at the Letetemetso blockage just south of Xugana. Here it splits to form the Moanachira and Khwai. The southerly fork runs into the Guekha, the Gomoti and the Santantabide rivers. Running at right angles to all of them at the base of the delta is the Thamalakane River, on which Maun is situated, and into which flow the Boro and the Santantadibe. At the height of the flood these rivers become diffused in the lagoons and flood-plains.

A boat is essential for getting around the delta's many islands and channels. The traditional canoe is the mokoro which, being dug out from a tree, is quite narrow and often has a bend in it. The first time I sat in one it felt very unstable, but you get used to it. A poler stands at the rear and steers the mokoro expertly through the carpet of waterlilies and papyrus. It is a very peaceful way of experiencing the delta, with only the gentle lapping of the water against the mokoro's flat wooden sides to distract you. You can hear all the sounds of the swamps as if you were part of them. Spending too long in a mokoro can be uncomfortable, though, for there is no room to move. As on any water, sunburn can be the biggest problem and a good broad-brimmed hat is essential. You must rely totally on the experience and vigilance of your poler, as the delta is full of hippo and crocodiles. Some people boast about swimming, and the crystal-clear water and sand banks look very inviting when you are hot, but really it is downright foolhardy.

We witnessed the fearful power of crocodiles in a remote lagoon, covered in the salvinia weed. The weed had nearly completely covered the water and, as it was the only water for some distance, there were many resident hippos and crocodiles, some of whom were enormous, measuring at least five metres in length.

During mid-morning, when the sand had warmed up, the crocodiles came out of the water and lay in the sun to raise their body temperatures. In the heat of the afternoon many animals came to drink. The impala were particularly nervous; some would not drink for many minutes as they tentatively approached the water, only to withdraw and then return again. Eventually their thirst overcame their fear of the crocodiles. Some of the antelopes had to walk within a few metres of the reptiles, basking on the edge of the lagoon, to get to the water.

Elephants and hippos had no such fear. They would quite obviously approach the basking crocodiles with the sole purpose of disturbing them.

It was while we watched this interaction that a great commotion attracted our attention on the other side of the lagoon. An impala had ventured too far into the salvinia-covered water. His flailing legs thrashing around, the ram was dragged under the green weed. Suddenly a great spiked tail rose out of the weed and slapped down into the water, throwing up a great cascade of mud. Soon crocodiles from all over the lagoon glided towards the scene, their reptilian scaled bodies twisted in the water exposing their yellow bellies.

One crocodile became entangled amongst the herd of hippos that were wallowing in the middle of the lagoon. The crocodile tried to escape over their backs, narrowly missing the lunging jaws of the dominant bull. Within minutes the feeding frenzy was over as the impala was ripped to pieces.

Being low in the water and quiet, a canoe offers the unique experience of being able to see a broad spectrum of wildlife, from water snakes and reed frogs to jacanas and herons. Then there is always the chance of sighting the rarely seen sitatunga, the shy, marsh-dwelling antelope that lives in the delta.

Crossing the many waterways of the Okavango Delta can be a tense business as you could be stranded a long way from any assistance. A winch and high-lift jack are strongly recommended.

On one mokoro trip we saw an African darter trying to swallow a squeaker. This is a small catfish that squeaks when alarmed and locks the bony spines on each of its dorsal fins to discourage its attacker from swallowing it. Cormorants and darters are usually experts in unlocking this defence, but this particular darter had failed to unhinge the spines properly, lodging the fish firmly in its mouth. It could neither swallow nor release the fish. The darter paid a high price for its miscalculation and eventually died with the rotting fish stuck in its throat.

The inhabitants of the delta are often referred to as River Bushmen. They are the baNoka people and they lived here long before the baYei spread south from the Zambezi. Livingstone observed that the different tribes were named after animals. The term baKatla means 'they of the monkey', the baKuena 'they of the crocodile' and the baTlapi 'they of the fish'. A single individual is indicated by the term mo. So a member of the baKwain tribe would be a moKwain. The personal pronoun 'they' is used extensively in the names of African tribes – ba, ma, wa, ova and so on.

Before independence, Botswana was called Bechuanaland. The name Bechuana could be derived from the word 'chua', which means 'alike' or 'equal'. Encompassing all the tribes of Bechuanaland as a generic term for the whole nation, it implies that there is no dominant tribe and that they are all equal in status.

The Moremi Game Reserve is less than 100 km from Maun, but the journey takes well over two hours. After passing through the veterinary cordon fence the road deteriorates. Soft sand, corrugation and deep ruts make maintaining

Klaas Smit's river-wagon broke down, crossing the drift. (*T. Baines*)

a constant speed impossible. Much of the journey is through dense mopane, interrupted on occasions by small flood-plains. It is well worth keeping your eyes open, for although this is outside the game reserve, it is still a wilderness area. We have seen lions, cheetahs, elephants and honey badgers along here. A large thatched roof over a barrier at South Gate marks the boundary of Moremi and from here we turned sharp left, past the public campsite.

During the winter months the herds leave the drying interior to the east for the more permanent waters of the delta. As we wound our way along the delta's edge, there were animals everywhere. Lush green marshes with towering palms fringed the lagoons where the crystal-clear water sparkled in the sunshine. Lechwe, in their hundreds, bobbed about in the tall reeds. At a relaxed pace we arrived at Xakanaxa lagoon four hours later and camped for the night.

The lagoon itself is not easily seen from the campsite, as the water is hidden by dense papyrus. Care should be taken as there are crocodiles around. Xakanaxa is in a very pleasant setting and the following day the campsite was to provide an encounter with Africa's rarest predators.

As we returned to camp the following evening, something caught my attention deep in the woods. A blur of patchwork colours darted amongst the trees. It was a pack of wild dogs. Within seconds they had disappeared into the woods again. This brief encounter served only to frustrate us, so, as it was getting dark, we decided to continue back to camp. As we drove into the campsite I was amazed to see the dogs again, chasing an impala ram between the tents. Several startled campers were taking refuge on a termite mound. There were dogs everywhere as they hounded the exhausted impala to the edge of the lagoon. There, a wall of papyrus confronted it and the terrified animal faltered. A moment's hesitation was all it took – one of the dogs grabbed its hind leg and pulled it to the ground. Within seconds the other dogs arrived and began to tear it apart. It was sad to see the death of one of these beautiful, elegant creatures, but I could only admire the ruthless determination of the wild dogs.

At this time of year the evenings turn cold as soon as the last warm rays of the sun disappear. I hadn't had time to build a fire and we were in our tent early that night when the first hyenas came into camp. Loud 'whoops' echoed amongst the trees, followed soon after by an excited cackle of laughter as the hyenas found the remains of the wild dogs' kill. It is not uncommon for hyenas to invade camp at night and we had been careful to leave not even a sandal lying around.

Frederick Selous described the call of the hyena as 'the most mournful and weird sound in nature'. Livingstone's companion, William Oswell, had a hatred of hyenas. He would chase them on horseback at full gallop, wielding his heavy stirrup over his head, and would kill the carnivore with one blow!

Hyenas do not have many admirers, but they are a vital part of the food chain. Each group, or clan, holds a territory which is fiercely defended against neighbouring clans. They scent-mark frequently along the borders of their territories, where disputes can result in savage battles.

In June, the hyenas give birth to their young. Their cubs are kept in communal dens, usually well hidden in the woodlands. There is a strict social hierarchy and some of the sub-adults are responsible for nursemaid duties while the rest of the clan go off to hunt.

One night we visited a den and were greeted by several young hyenas which ran up to us inquisitively. Like all predators, they are naturally curious and explored around the vehicle, showing great interest in the tyres, which they tried to deflate with their strong little jaws.

Apart from Xakanaxa, there are three other public campsites in Moremi: at South Gate, Third Bridge and North Gate, Khwai, where elephants frequently wander through the camp rearranging the trees!

The Khwai is one of the delta's fingertips, a small tributary that in recent years has enjoyed good floods. It cuts a wedge between the mopane woodlands of Moremi and a Controlled Hunting Area. Once across the river and its broad flood-plains there is no permanent water until you reach the great rivers of the north. The Khwai also marks the northern boundary of the Moremi Game Reserve. During September the floodwaters reach this extremity of the delta and the river rises rapidly, seeping well into the Chobe National Park, which shares Moremi's eastern boundary. In the mopane the pans were almost dry and the wildlife concentrated along the Khwai in increasing numbers. As the days got hotter, and with the rains still more than two months away, the need for the animals to drink increased. The bushes and trees were bare as the dry season tightened its grip.

Miraculously, the water was rising throughout the delta as the flood continued to flow down. Large herds of elephants appeared, running from the woodlands in eager anticipation of the refreshing water that awaited them. The reflection of the clear blue sky turned the colour of the water to a vivid deep blue that contrasted with the dry golden grass that surrounded it.

Breeding herds of elephants are always nervous as they approach the river and are not relaxed in the presence of vehicles. Thoughtless tourists who try to get too close can frighten them away. Sometimes a calf may linger to savour one more drink and an inexperienced young cow may lose it in the confusion. Without its mother to guard it a lonely calf will be surely lost to lions or hyenas.

We had moved our camp from Xakanaxa to Khwai. During our time in Moremi we acquired a tent on one of our frequent visits to Maun where we restocked with food and fuel. We had decided to set up a more permanent camp at Khwai. Although not as pretty as Xakanaxa, the campsite was close to the excellent game viewing areas of the Khwai floodplains. The campsite is opposite a village which is situated out of the reserve beyond the bridge at

Fed by rains in the Angolan highlands, the water of the Okavango river takes six months to reach the southern edge of the delta. At a time when rain-filled pans are drying up wildlife turns to the delta's flood, an oasis in the dry Kalahari.

OPPOSITE: *Fresh floodwater fills the Okavango Delta. The blue water makes a stark contrast to the dry yellow grass.*

North Gate. Here the villages, of bushman origin, live much the same as they did in Livingstone's time. Only the style of dress has changed in that they wear European clothes. Their dwellings are simple thatched rondavels made from mud. An interesting innovation has been the addition of tin cans which are built into the walls.

OPPOSITE:
Herds of a thousand or more can still be seen but overall numbers of buffalo in the Okavango have dropped alarmingly according to recent surveys.

A juvenile martial eagle, a hunter of small birds and rodents, soars over the delta wetlands.

The dust from roaming buffalo herds can be seen from miles away.

A bull hippo (Hippopotamus amphibius) displays his awesome jaws in a remote lagoon on the fringe of the delta. The surface is covered in salvinia weed which, if left unchecked, will spread rapidly, choking the waterways of aquatic life.

A group of impala approach the crocodile infested lagoon nervously and with good reason.

An impala that ventured too far. It failed to notice the crocodiles lying amongst the salvinia until it was too late. The water explodes in fury as the impala is dragged under by the massive jaws.

Soon crocodiles from all over the lagoon are attracted by the commotion and join in a feeding frenzy, twisting their bodies to tear the animal apart.

Dust hangs in the air amongst Hyphaene palms as a herd of wildebeest rest on a dry lagoon.

The spoonbill stork (Platalea alba) prefers fresh water, frequenting swamps, lakes and rivers.

The white-fronted bee-eater (Merops bullockoides) is mainly found in eastern parts of southern Africa but is also widespread in the Okavango.

A female sitatunga (Tragelaphus spekei) delicately leaps across a lagoon. These shy animals will hide in dense papyrus or under water with only their nose protruding, when threatened.

The Moremi Game Reserve provides sanctuary for a wide variety of wildlife, including a healthy population of Africa's rarest predator: the African Wild Dog (Lycaon pictus) or painted wolf.

A pack of wild dogs cross into the Moremi Game Reserve over a shallow part of the Khwai river.

Chapter Three
The Wild Dogs of Moremi

(*Colophospermum mopane*) – *mopane*

The time we spent at Khwai was incredible for its encounters with wild dogs. We frequently saw three different packs and on one morning when we chose to stay in camp, they visited us, chasing an impala through the campsite!

We had met researchers John (Tico) McNutt and Lesley Boggs on a previous trip. At that time we had been using Polaroids to try and identify the dogs. We learned from Tico that each dog is uniquely marked and so adopted his method of identifying individuals by sketching the rump and tail of each dog. This made our experience with them much more meaningful.

Moremi is perhaps the best area in Botswana for observing wild dogs, where they are regularly seen along the flood-plains of the Khwai. There are at least ten packs in Tico's study-area in and around the Moremi tongue and, remarkably, he knows each and every individual. During June and July the dogs have their pups and, with Tico's help, we located the site of one of the dens, in the mopane. Each pack had a name and we were watching 'the Party pack'. All the dogs had been given names of a beer or cider. It is essential to be able to recognise each dog and the weeks we spent watching the pups grow were most rewarding. For the mother, Harp, it was her fifth litter of her six years and she tirelessly tended to her demanding pups. All the nine members of the pack took a great interest, in particular two yearlings from Harp's previous litter: a female called Sail and a male, Griffin, who was nearly entirely blond. Perhaps the least interested was Fetch, the father. Throughout the day the adults remained at the den and took turns in regurgitating meat to satisfy the voracious appetites of the youngsters. Hunting took place during the twilight hours before sunrise and after sunset and on moonlit nights. Usually one or two dogs remained behind while the pups spent the night inside the den.

It was always an exciting moment to watch the dogs race back to the den, where they would be greeted with great excitement and twittering from the pups.

Wild dogs show great care and affection to one another and always have time for their young. When they are old enough to go on hunts, they allow them to feed first.

Wild dogs have unjustly been called violent killers and vermin, but they are no worse than any other predator. They hunt mainly impala, lechwe, reedbuck and steenbok but will take the young of larger antelope like wildebeest, tsessebe or kudu.

We have actually heard a tourist ask if they are domestic dogs gone wild! Lycaon Pictus is a species of the family canidae and unique to Africa where, sadly, it is endangered. Like the wolf it is only tolerated by man in protected areas. If it strays from these areas it is likely to be shot by farmers. If you are lucky enough to see one, look at its beautiful markings. Perfect camouflage for the mopane woodlands, where it spends much of its time.

The days in Moremi were getting longer and hotter, but the mornings were still cold, even after the first rays of the sun had penetrated through the trees to touch the wild dogs' den.

This was a cue for the pups to emerge. One by one they would scramble up the steep sandy entrance and huddle together for warmth in a sunny spot between the long shadows of the early morning.

One or two of the adults, or yearlings, would usually stay behind and watch over the youngsters. Their large round ears constantly twitched as they tried to identify any unusual sounds. If they were unsure they would stand up and stare intently towards the source of their interest.

Once a pair of jackals trotted out of the bushes, unaware of the dogs' presence. Instantly the yearling dog, Griffin, the blond male, stood up and gave a short bark, an alarm call that instantly sent the pups scurrying back down into the den. The jackals, however, had no wish to hang around either and went on their way as Griffin stood to confront them.

The pups, at six weeks, never went far from the den when the pack was away. There was always a possibility that lions or hyenas might stumble across the den in the early morning and that would have been a very different scenario.

The pack would sometimes return at sunrise, or three hours later, depending on the length of the hunt. The guarding dog and pups always alerted us as

Racing back to the den, three members of the pack return from a successful hunt.

soon as the first of the returning dogs approached and there would be great excitement as they ran to greet them. With faces stained red from their kill, the hunters raced back to the den. The waiting dogs were eager to see that all had returned safely as they excitedly greeted each other. Then, one by one, they would regurgitate fresh meat and be enveloped in a mêlée of hungry pups as their high-pitched twittering excited the adults who would run around, playfully bowling the youngsters over.

Once the initial excitement had died down, the dogs would lie down under the trees or bushes near the den. The pups would be active for quite some time, chasing one another for scraps or having a tug of war. As they grew older their games became increasingly rougher.

Until the pups were fully weaned, their mother, Harp, usually stayed behind and would also take meat by encouraging the hunters to regurgitate for her. The bond that exists between members of a pack is very strong and is important for their survival.

Harp's pack consisted of nine adults, plus her ten pups. Fetch was the alpha male and not related to Harp who was the dominant breeding female. The rest of the members included brothers and sisters and offspring from previous litters. Some of the offspring might stay for as long as two or three years with their natal pack before joining another or forming a new pack of their own.

Although nine to twelve is a common number, we did see one pack from the Chitabe area with twenty-six dogs. One pack at Third Bridge was recorded with over forty!

One morning we arrived at the den to find the pack had already killed. Something was different that day and the pups were running around in one group. One by one the dogs trotted off in a line with all ten pups in tow. We had noticed that the pups, now eight weeks old, would try to follow the adults on hunts, much to their irritation, but on this particular morning they had already killed. It was obvious they were moving to another den site and we were in for a bumpy ride through the trees.

Four km later, and with the help of the tracking equipment Tico had lent me, we arrived at the new den. It had probably been excavated originally by an aardvark. There were five entrances with a very deep one with a steep sandy slope. Harp descended into this hole to inspect their new home while the pups stood in line above, peering expectantly down at their mother, awaiting her approval.

This was one of many sites that Harp had within her territory and had been used in previous years. Before taking the pups there it is probable that the dogs had investigated the site while out hunting, to make sure it was not occupied by hyenas or porcupines.

There was a den at Khwai which porcupines actually shared with hyenas, and three days earlier we had witnessed a porcupine occupying Harp's den which may have precipitated her move.

On that morning there were only five pups in evidence, and the dogs, Harp and her yearling daughter, Sail, in particular, were greatly distressed.

They repeatedly went down into the entrance, whining and whimpering, occasionally going right inside, which would be followed by a strange wurring sound from within. It was then we realized there was a porcupine inside and this noise was from the animal shaking its quills as it obviously felt threatened by the agitated dogs. The other five pups must have been trapped in one or two of the chambers.

This performance went on throughout the day as Harp became increasingly stressed. However, her persistence paid off later in the day when the first three pups emerged, followed at sunset by the last two. All looked very relieved that their ordeal was over and needless to say they were ravenous. That night all the pups had to remain outside the den and, interestingly, none of the dogs went off to hunt.

The butterfly leaves of the Mopane tree turn to gold in July. This time of year is when the wild dogs are rearing their pups at selected den sites in their favoured habitat, the mopane woodlands. At five weeks the pups are out of the den. Apart from the white patches, their coats are dark. In the cold winter mornings they huddle together for warmth.

'Sail', a yearling female, watches over the pups at the den while the rest of the pack are away hunting.

It is the fifth litter for the pups' six-year-old mother, Harp, and they are forever demanding of milk.

We did not see the porcupine leave the den during the night but it had definitely gone by the following morning. Two days later, after Harp had moved to the new den, we found two porcupine quills in the main tunnel.

The pups grew quickly and within a few weeks they were no longer the little black bundles we had first seen. Their tan markings had come through and by September they were ready to leave the dens for good and follow the pack. It would be from this time that they would be most at risk when they would be more likely to encounter other predators at kills. Lions do not tolerate wild dogs any more than other competitors and will kill them.

A few weeks later, after we had left Moremi, we learned from Tico that two of the pups had died and Fetch had broken his hind leg, although he was still with the pack.

It seemed that an era was over for Harp's pack as it would be unlikely that Fetch would father any future litters. Harp herself was getting old, the average longevity of Lycaon Pictus in the wild is four to five years. For the rest of the pack – Sail, Griffin, Tetley, Newcky, Scrumpy, Singha, Fyxx and the surviving pups – the order was about to change.

The pups are greeted with great affection and enthusiasm after the adults return from hunting.

'Fetch', the pups' father, adopts the typical hunting poise which is also a signal to the pups that he is prepared to regurgitate.

'Fyxx' brings up great chunks of meat, which the pups energetically fight over.

. . .this often leads to a tug of war . . .

Early one morning the pack suddenly left the den, with all ten pups in tow. The dogs rarely stayed at a den for longer than twelve days before moving to another selected site within their territory.

'Harp' inspects the new den while some of the pups line up, anxiously awaiting her approval. They had travelled four kilometres from the old den.

Three pups bask in the early morning sunshine. At nine weeks their tan markings are showing through.

Hooded vultures (Necrosyntes monachus) were often in attendance, picking up left-over scraps. To the pups these were strange creatures that always attracted their curiosity.

At four months the young dogs are old enough to follow the pack. It is from this time that they are at the greatest risk from other predators such as lions and hyenas.

Usually wild dogs live in harmony and show great affection to one another. In a rare moment of aggression two males dispute the right over access to an oestrus female.

The water evaporated quickly in the hot October sun, and countless sips from birds and animals, large and small, eventually turned parts of the Khwai into treacherous pools of mud.

Beyond the flood-plains, the vast mopane woodlands were grey and bare, shadeless and hot. The red carpet of dry mopane leaves crackled under the feet of wandering elephants who left a trail of fallen trees in their wake. The contrast of the dry interior was stark as the grey woodlands gave way to yellow grassy plains that ran down to lush green marshes along the river. During the hot afternoons many species of animals joined the resident lechwe, reedbuck and waterbuck. Sable, roan, kudu and giraffe, tsessebe and wildebeest, zebras, impalas, elephants and baboons. At sunset, like a swarm of locusts, queleas descended to drink and, as darkness fell, they would roost in the trees and bushes. Civets and servals took advantage of this and frequently caught the tiny birds.

With the abundance of predators, the impala in particular were being taken regularly and they formed into large groups. It was not only the wild dogs who were successful. The leopards used stealth and cunning, while the cheetahs used their tremendous acceleration and speed to run them down In Botswana's savannah woodlands cheetahs have large home ranges.

Along the upper reaches of the Khwai, the floodwater had pushed right into the Chobe and great numbers of animals were moving in during September, including two prides of lions. One pride consisted of nineteen which included several adult lionesses, cubs and sub-adults, led by a large dark-maned lion.

This pride rarely moved beyond a 5-km stretch of river close to Mochaba Camp. Further up the Khwai, just inside the boundary of the Chobe National Park, was another pride of seven. In contrast the dominant male was a beautiful blond-maned lion.

The days were never dull at Khwai. Despite the heat that intensified each day, the regular visits of elephants in camp kept us entertained.

One day a large bull walked right up to our tent and stopped a few paces from where I was sitting. After standing motionless for a few minutes he rubbed his back nonchalantly against a small tree nearby. Then he casually ambled off, swinging his head from side to side.

A close encounter with an elephant was suitably described by Thomas Baines: '. . . If anyone wants to know what it is like let him take a black mass of anything, the bigger and more shapeless the better, then still further obscure it with a cloud of dust and he will have a tolerable idea of the reality.'

Every day the elephants would demolish yet another tree in the campsite, depleting the already scant canopy of shade. The baboons and vervet monkeys needed extra vigilance however. They were ever-present and a constant pest, always watching for an opportunity to steal some food the moment your back was turned. One large male had no fear at all of women and on more than one occasion threatened Maggi when she was alone. Everything had to be secured in the mess tent when we left camp.

OPPOSITE: *Although not good climbers, cheetahs use fallen trees as a vantage point to observe the landscape.*

OPPOSITE: *The cheetah's legendary speed will only take it over short distances. In woodland areas it is always at risk of injury from pot-holes, logs and thorns.*

Two young male cheetahs (Acinonyx jubata) drink from a water-hole in Moremi. In semi-desert areas they can survive without water, gaining liquid from their prey.

An impala is pulled down. The cheetah must devour its meal quickly as competitors like hyena, lion or leopard will chase it off, if discovered. After the chase the cheetah can take up to five minutes before feeding while it gets its breath back. During this time it nervously looks around for other predators. Cheetahs are mainly diurnal, but in open areas like the Kalahari, they will hunt on moonlit nights.

OPPOSITE: *One afternoon an elephant bull wandered into our camp on the Khwai.*

Tin cans are recycled to build mud huts. Nowadays a common feature in building the walls.

OPPOSITE: *The children enjoyed dressing-up for dancing. The skirts were made from plastic sacking.*

BELOW LEFT: *Although the local lodges employ some of the villagers, antelope are still hunted for subsistence. Here the meat is hung up to dry after skinning.*

BELOW: *Cooking on an open log fire.*

Rivers like the Khwai start to fill with water flowing down from the delta. The surrounding plains resemble fields of wheat in golden hues.

Easily distinguished by its red beak and short stubby tail, the Bateleur (Terathopius ecandatus) is one of the most striking of the raptors. It favours open flood plains and savannah woodland.

A saddlebill stork (Ephippiorhynchus senegalensis) struggles to direct a large fish down its long bill. Fish eagles sometimes seize an opportunity like this to steal an easy meal.

The call of the lilac breasted roller (Coracias candata) is a series of harsh chirps. The bird likes to perch on good vantage points from where it will suddenly descend to the ground to take a grasshopper or some other insect. Its wings are a brilliant blue when spread during flight.

Black-backed jackals (Canis mesomelas) find small birds, like red-eyed doves, are easy prey at the water's edge.

OPPOSITE: *The jackals had hungry pups to feed. They encouraged the parents to regurgitate food by licking the adult's mouth and yelping excitedly.*

Adorned with a feather from its last meal, an alert pup waited for its parents to return to the den.

He was a magnificent lion (Panthera leo), bearing the scars of battle. In August a pride of 19 lions, led by this large male, moved into the Khwai from the Mobabe.

Red-billed queleas (Quelia quelia) began to appear along the Khwai in huge numbers.

A bushbaby (Galago senegalensis) made a regular appearance in Mochaba camp at night. Strictly nocturnal, their large wide eyes give them excellent night vision enabling them to make remarkable leaps among the trees.

Two giraffe bulls (Giraffa camelopardalis) engaged in a necking contest, occasionally delivering a powerful head blow under the chest.

OPPOSITE: *Within a couple of weeks the trees had lost their leaves as the Khwai crept further into the Chobe.*

A beautiful young leopard (Panthera pardus) crouched to drink from the fresh flowing water . . .

. . . then, in one bound, leapt to the other side.

OPPOSITE: *The young male leopard was relaxing in one of his favourite trees.*

The leopard caught an impala ram and was holding him by the throat, choking the antelope till it died.

CHAPTER FOUR
THE LINYANTI AND SAVUTI MARSHES

(Ficus Sycomorus) – Mochaba – Sycamore Fig

We struck camp early and left Khwai for Savuti.

The Moremi woodlands looked very different now to when we had arrived. However, with the dry season at its height, the acacias were blossoming. The small yellow buds were a delight for the giraffes. As we drove along the Khwai for the last time, we came across two male giraffes necking. Like all antelope, young bulls like to test their strength and practise for the day when they will assert their dominance. The mature giraffe bulls are much darker and easily distinguishable from the sub-adults.

The two young bulls swung back and forth, their long necks swaying gracefully like swans in some exotic dance. Occasionally a well-aimed swing from one of the combatants landed a loud thud on its opponent, who would jump at the moment of impact. We watched, entranced, for half an hour.

As we travelled north, towards Savuti, we crossed a particularly soft section of sand. We were on the Magwikwe sand ridge, which is believed to be the ancient northern shoreline of the great lake of Makgadikgadi. The sand ridge curves sharply around two groups of rocky hills, Gubatsaa and Goha, which are north of the Savuti Marsh. The ridge then sweeps south-east along the edge of the Mababe depression.

Goha can be seen clearly dominating the horizon from some distance away and when Livingstone passed it in 1851 he wrote about the hill he called N'gwa, 'This being the only hill we had seen since leaving Bamangwato,[1] we felt inclined to take our hats off to it. It is three or four hundred feet high, and covered with trees.'

The Mababe Depression, as its name implies, is a low-lying flat plain of black cotton soil. This was the bed of the ancient lake and, after seasonal rains, its nutritious grass attracts large herds of zebra. Three dry river channels cut gaps through the sand ridge around the Savuti Marsh: the Ngwezumba lies to the east, and the Tsatsarra on the western ridge. The third channel, the Savuti, has a varied history, but has been dry since 1981. It winds its way down from Linyanti, and has been an erratic watercourse since James Chapman crossed it in 1853. It was dry then, too, but nearly twenty years later the hunter Frederick Courtney Selous noted that the Savuti Channel was full. In 1880 it

OPPOSITE: *Bare of leaves, the trees offered no concealment to birds like the martial eagle (Polemaetus bellicosus).*

1. In South Africa.

Photography under difficulties. Chapman's 'Travels in the Interior of S.A.' (1868).

dried up again until 1956, when once again the channel flowed. Until 1981 there were spectacular concentrations of animals, including resident hippos, crocodiles and waterbuck. Then, once again, the water deserted Savuti. In the harsh dry season of 1982 the river that the animals depended on turned to mud. The tragedy was graphically recorded in the Jouberts' film *The Stolen River*.

Lying on fault lines at the southern end of the Great Rift Valley, this area is prone to seismic activity. Even subtle movements can change the course of rivers or affect the gradients enough to prevent them flowing.

In October Savuti was a dry and dusty place. The only water was at a pumped waterhole nearby[2] and in the ablution blocks and taps around the campsite. During our stay the pump broke down and as the waterhole dried up the elephants became irritable and aggressive. Some came into camp and tried to get water from the showers, pulling out pipes in the process.

The Savuti Marsh was bone dry and the grass held little nourishment for the few tsessebe that remained. Clouds bubbled up in the hot afternoons as warm winds blew up dust-devils that danced across the plains. For the lions of Savuti it was a difficult time. The zebra had all left for the delta and Linyanti, and we, too, decided to move on.

Shortly after leaving Savuti the road north to Kasane passes the Goha Hills. At a crossroads there we turned left and headed north-west along a cut-line track that within an hour and a half brought us to the edge of the Linyanti Marsh. This section is the extreme western corner of the Chobe National Park.

In 1857 the Linyanti was the scene of a tragedy involving the first expedition of missionaries funded by the London Missionary Society. The idea had been proposed by Livingstone after he had established relations with the Makololo tribe who lived there. The objective was to move the tribe from the malaria-infested swamps to the higher ground of the Batoka Plateau near the Victoria Falls, far to the east. The expedition was led by Helmore and Price and they understood that Livingstone would be at the village of the Makololo to meet them. Livingstone had been a friend of the chief, Sekeletu, for six years and the missionaries deemed it safe enough to bring their wives and children. However, the venture had been built on totally optimistic expectations, most of which were Livingstone's. He had no intention of being at Linyanti at this time,

2. Since this was written the Department of Wildlife has opened two more pumped waterholes in Savuti.

being busy exploring the Zambezi beyond the Victoria Falls. Chief Sekeletu was upset that the doctor had not returned with his guides nor brought the ivory that had been promised, and he had no sympathy for the people that Livingstone had sent to him. Helmore and Price had no experience in dealing with Africans and many of the party were already falling sick within weeks of their arrival.

The Makololo used the missionaries' plight to deprive them of their possessions, and within two months Mr and Mrs Helmore, Mrs Price and five children were dead. It was later speculated that they had been poisoned, but it is more likely they died from malaria. As the grief-stricken Roger Price and the two surviving children attempted to leave, Sekeletu took away one of their wagons. So, with only the food they could carry to sustain them, Price and the children embarked on the long trek home. They were fortunate to meet up with Bishop Mackenzie, who should have been with the original party, but had departed late and was on his way to join them.

(Hippotragus niger) A solitary sable bull drinks from a peaceful lagoon. The majestic antelope will often drink during the heat of the day when there is less risk from predators.

History has put much of the blame for the tragedy on Livingstone. His presence at Linyanti would surely have made for acceptance of the missionaries, but perhaps most bewildering of all was that Livingstone never recommended the use of quinine as a cure for malaria before the party had set out, knowing as he did its effectiveness and the danger that malaria would pose. Livingstone discredited himself by putting the blame on the shoulders of others, including the London Missionary Society, for not sending out a doctor with the expedition. The reality was that the LMS had assumed the doctor of the expedition would be Livingstone!

The irony of the tragedy was that had Sekeletu co-operated with the missionaries, the Makololo themselves might have been saved. When Livingstone did return in 1860, he found many of them had died from fever. With only fifty true Makololo left, Sekeletu's rule would be soon over when the subjugated Barotse people massacred them in an uprising.

Today there are no Makololo, or any villages for that matter, along Linyanti, except in the northern salient at Kachikau. Most of Linyanti has been set aside for hunting and photographic safaris. It is still a remote place, though, and the weeks we spent there were among the most pleasurable of our journey.

Driving along the narrow, twisting, sandy track through the woodlands along the Linyanti must be done with care. The elephant breeding herds here are particularly aggressive. One afternoon we found ourselves struggling through a soft section of deep sand, when suddenly a large herd appeared around a sharp bend. Two of the leading females immediately adopted a threatening posture, raising their heads, spreading their ears and trumpeting loudly. Behind them young calves scurried across the track into the trees. The matriarch was very agitated and I decided to reverse quietly around the bend. The gearbox, however, whined loudly as the wheels found traction in the soft sand. I had only retreated a few metres when I heard a loud crack from behind. I had come within metres of another herd crossing behind us. There was no alternative but to sit it out, so I switched off the engine in case the noise disturbed them further. Having seen their young safely across, the herds went their separate ways and we were suddenly alone. It is not uncommon for vehicles to be attacked by nervous elephants who make it clear you are not welcome.

The devastation to the woodlands along the Linyanti resembled the aftermath of a battle, with dead and decaying wood scattered around.

As we drove further along the edge of the Linyanti towards the mouth of the Savuti Channel, we had our first encounter with tsetse flies. The tsetse has nearly been eradicated from Botswana, but along the Linyanti it seemed to be making a comeback, and the further south we went the more numerous they became. Nobody can pretend to enjoy their company, for the fly is persistent in its attempts to bite. Conservationists welcome them as a protector of wildlife, for cattle cannot survive in tsetse-fly country. The insect is prominent in the company of buffalo and the Linyanti is buffalo country.

We crossed the old log bridge over the Savuti Channel and followed the watercourse for a few kilometres out on to the large, flat plains of the Selinda Spillway. This is one of Botswana's remote frontiers. On the other side of the Linyanti lies the Caprivi strip in Namibia, from where poachers can easily cross over. Fortunately there is less activity now since the war in Namibia ended, and the security forces have mostly been successful in minimizing these incursions.

Beyond the vast mopane woodlands lie the perennial waterways of Linyanti, as vital to wildlife as the delta itself. From the Linyanti winds the Savuti channel that used to feed a wildlife paradise called the Savuti marsh. Now it is dry.

Burchell's zebra (Equus Burchellii) are generally whiter than their northern cousins and show a shadow stripe. Many of these zebra make the long journey from Savuti to the woodlands of Linyanti, where they will be close to water during the dry season. However zebra numbers have dropped alarmingly during the last decade and research has yet to show the reason for this.

Some of the zebra from Savuti make their way here during the dry season, but, like all areas in Botswana, it is seasonal. One month the plains may be alive with animals, the next there may be nothing at all.

The Selinda Spillway, or Magwagqana as it is also known, is in a controlled hunting area and at the end of the hunting season in September the game can be very skittish. The sound of a motor is enough to send the herds into panic. Even the lions are shy and avoid contact with vehicles. The flat plains are dotted with large termite mounds, many of which support small trees. Clusters of palms, reminiscent of the Makgadikgadi, help to break up what is a rather featureless landscape, through which the spillway winds and curves, taking water from the Okavango into the Linyanti. It has been observed that, in some years, the spillway can be seen to flow in the opposite direction, but, as the Linyanti is lower than the delta, it is more likely explained as being a backwash of water.

A zebra rolls in the dust to rid itself of biting flies.

The long drive back to Savuti through the mopane was monotonous, broken only by large areas that had been blackened by bush fires. Sometimes these fires are started intentionally in cattle areas to encourage new growth. They can spread rapidly, fanned by the strong October winds.

The Gubatsaa Hills at Savuti are unusual in that there are very few rocky features in this part of Botswana. There are small caves, which once gave shelter to the Bushmen. Their artwork still remains on some rocks overlooking the Savuti Channel to remind us of their previous residents. The rocks also provide a home for leopards.

We had been driving around the hills one afternoon hoping to find one of these elusive cats. Straining to search under every bush and in every tree can be quite tiring on the eyes and we have been fooled by logs with ears many times! I stopped the Toyota. An image had registered in my mind in a clump of bushes we had just passed. I was sure there was something there, but if it was a cat, it was a very small one. Maybe a wild cat.

We both peered through our binoculars after I had pointed the bush out to Maggi. A small grey shape lay underneath, quite still, in the shadows. The dry grass concealed it as I strained to identify what I was beginning to think was indeed a small cat.

'It's a baby leopard,' I whispered.

'Yes, I see it,' Maggi replied, 'but it's got something.'

I switched on the motor and carefully edged forward, stopping again after a few metres. I reckoned I needed to get at least another 10 metres closer if the cat was going to fill the frame of my 600mm lens, but better to try and get something than nothing. As quietly as possible I raised myself through the roof hatch and fixed the camera with its heavy lens to the tripod head I had clamped on the roof. The powerful lens zoomed into focus. The leopard cub was staring straight at me. A little bundle of fur with large dark spots and wild yellow eyes. His chin and whiskers were bright red with fresh blood. His upper lip quivered and then broke into a snarl. The cub held his ground for beneath him was his prize. It was the foetus of an impala, freshly killed. The body of the dead female impala lay beside the cub, but where was the cub's own mother? She must be close by. At that moment the cub took the rump of the foetus in his little jaws and started to drag the equally small carcass backwards. Every now and then he tripped, but he was very determined that we were not going to have any of his meal.

The rock kopjes at the northern end of Savuti are ideal leopard haunts. Cubs are usually born in caves or holes in the ground.

OPPOSITE: *The mother moves her cubs to a new den every few days to minimise the risk of detection from other predators.*

A leopard cub can eat solid food when six weeks old. In October many of the impala are pregnant and we watched a cub feeding on the foetus pulled from a dead impala, killed by the leopard's mother.

By this time the sun was casting long, dark shadows across the scene. The difference in exposure between light and shade was making my camera give erratic readings. Shortly after sunset, the cub's mother appeared. In the twilight she began to drag the half-eaten impala towards some thick bushes. Although there were no suitable trees nearby, I wondered why she hadn't taken her kill off to a safer place, because hyenas would surely find her here.

A few days later we saw her again, carrying the cub in her jaws beneath the tall boulders of one of the kopjes. They sat together for a while before disappearing into the bushes.

In 1851 Oswell, Livingstone, his wife Mary and their three children trekked through the barren dry mopane forests near the Mababe Depression. Their Bushman guide, Shobo, had deserted them and their water was nearly finished:

> . . . the only vegetation was low scrub in deep sand; not a bird or insect enlivened the landscape. It was without exception the most uninviting prospect I ever beheld. . . . The supply of water had been wasted by one of the servants and by the afternoon only a small portion remained for the children . . . the idea of their perishing before our eyes was terrible.

The expedition might have ended in disaster had they not been lucky enough to find a pan that still held some water. They were 100 km from the Chobe River.

PREVIOUS PAGE and LEFT: *Just across the Chobe boundary a blond male mated regularly with a lioness for over a week. These amorous encounters were often accompanied by a lot of snarling.*

RIGHT and BELOW: *One lioness in the pride had two cubs that constantly harassed her for milk . . . she usually relented.*

OPPOSITE: *Climbing a termite mound, a young cub invited challenges from the other youngsters.*

In the cool of early morning, the lions often played down by the river.

PREVIOUS PAGES: *The cubs usually stayed close to their mothers.*

The lions frequently crossed the Khwai, preferring not to get wet.

A baby elephant, separated from its mother was killed by the blond-maned lion . . .

. . . he guarded his kill for two days.

His pride never went far from the river.

Famous for its lions, the Savuti marsh is a dry floodplain for much of the year. On the horizon the Gobatsaa Hills are a prominent feature.

OPPOSITE: *A pair of Bat-eared foxes (Otocyon megalotis) have a den out on the plain. The large ears of the fox enable it to detect insects underground. Their main diet is termites and scorpions and although it will eat meat, its weak jaws restrict it to eating only small creatures.*

The pups were eager to suckle when the mother returned from foraging.

The long tongue of a kudu (Tragelaphus strepsiceros) delicately pulls the last remaining leaves from the dry bush.

OPPOSITE: *An elephant bull, his parched skin reflecting the red glow of the setting sun, quenches his thirst from a drying pan.*

An impressive display from an elephant intended to intimidate 'Egret'.

The pump at Savuti's waterhole had broken down, leaving the birds and animals confused and thirsty.

PREVIOUS PAGE: *The elephants became irritable and frequent fights broke out.*

Often making its own kills, the spotted hyena (Crocuta crocuta) hunt in large clans at Savuti. They have incredibly strong jaws which are able to chew bones and carry off large pieces from a carcass.

They will intimidate other predators, like cheetah, to abandon their kills.

Pangolins (Manis temminckii) can sometimes be seen setting out to forage before dark. Moving on its hind legs, it occasionally touches the ground with its forefeet, the powerful claws of which are used to dig open termite mounds or nests of other insects on which it feeds.

OPPOSITE: *The mopane merges with camelthorn and wild teak and comes to an abrupt end at the edge of the Linyanti.*

The Magwagqana, or more commonly known as the Selinda Spillway, is an overflow from the Okavango Panhandle. The channel snakes its way across the floodplains on its way to meet the Linyanti.

Red lechwe (Kobus leche) are common, finding refuge in the perennial swamps.

Hippo help to keep the channels open through the swamps.

OPPOSITE: *An elephant lazily crosses one of Linyanti's large lagoons.*

The sitatunga is a relative of the kudu and the bulls are prized for their spiral horns. Its long, splayed hooves enable it to run through the spongy reedbeds.

Tranquillity and remoteness. The Linyanti is not a common destination for many visitors and has changed little since the time of Livingstone.

The evocative cry of the fish eagle, with head thrown back, can be heard on nearly every bend of the river.

PREVIOUS PAGE: *Zebra kinship groups have a dominant stallion who guards his mares aggressively against intruders. A stallion affectionately greets his favourite mare.*

OPPOSITE: *A darter (Anhinga melanogaster) had a squeaker stuck in its throat. As the fish had locked its bony pectoral spines, the bird choked to death.*

A fish eagle (Haliaeetus vocifer) swooped low over a lagoon and, with precision timing, took an unsuspecting barbel from the water.

With great beats from its wings the eagle lifted the fish clear of the water.

A boomslang (Dispholidus typus) reveals its deadly fangs. Although seldom seen there are plenty about. Like most reptiles it hibernates during the cold months of winter.

CHAPTER FIVE
THE CHOBE, THE ZAMBEZI AND THE DISCOVERY OF THE VICTORIA FALLS

(Adansonia Digitata) –
Mowane –
Baobab

The long drive up through the Chobe can be tedious, along a well-used sand track that in places is very slow going. The mopane forests seemed to thin out in parts, only to return again, kilometre after kilometre. We drove through little villages – Kachikau, Kavimba and Mabele – and finally arrived at Ngoma Bridge. Stretched out before us were the wide flood-plains of the Chobe River.

It was on 18 June 1851 that the first Europeans beheld this great river, where an emissary of the Makololo king, Sebituane (Sekeletu's predecessor), waited to greet them. Livingstone and Oswell left Mary and the children with the wagons and were taken 20 km downstream in a canoe to meet the great warrior.

William Cotton Oswell described the warm welcome they received at Seshéke:

> Presently this really great chief and man came to meet us, shy and ill at ease. We held out our hands in the accustomed way of true Britons and were surprised to see that his motherwit gave him immediate insight into what was expected of him, and the friendly meaning of our salutation. Though he could have never witnessed it before, he at once followed suit and placed his hand in ours as if to the manner born. I felt troubled at the evident nervousness of the famous warrior. Surrounded by his tribesmen he stood irresolute and quite overcome in the presence of two ordinary-looking Englishmen. . . .

Livingstone added:

> He was upon an island with all his principal men around him, and engaged in singing when we arrived. It was more like church music . . . and they continued for some seconds after we approached. . . .

Sebituane had led the Makololo from the region of Kuruman, which is near the present South African border with Botswana. His tribe had been attacked by the Griquas in 1824 and fled north where, in a succession of further attacks, first by Boers and then by the Matabele Zulus, they crossed the Kalahari by nearly the same path that Livingstone and Oswell had followed. Eventually Sebituane settled on the Zambezi and conquered all the people up to the Kafue, in modern Zambia. However, he was still being threatened from the east. The Ndebele, another Zulu tribe under Mzilikazi, were a warlike people who not only attacked Sebituane on more than one occasion, but were also the enemies of all their neighbours. Sebituane was anxious for the security of his people after years of upheaval and he knew that Livingstone's father-in-law, Robert Moffat, was a good friend of Mzilikazi. Through Livingstone, Sebituane therefore hoped for an eventual peace.

Oswell wrote of how, that first night, Sebituane visited him and Livingstone and recounted the history of his life, talking till dawn. It had pleased Sebituane that Livingstone had shown confidence in him by bringing along his children. However, this was the last time he took his family. He sent them back to England soon after, and hardly ever saw them again.

Shortly after this famous meeting, Sebituane died of a lung infection. Livingstone was with his son, Robert, at the chief's deathbed. He wrote:

> After sitting with him some time and commending him to the mercy of God, I rose to depart, when the dying chieftain raising himself up a little from his prone position called a servant and said, 'Take Robert to Maunku [one of his wives] and tell her to give him some milk.' These were the last words of Sebituane. . . .

There followed a period of uncertainty, but Livingstone and Oswell's party were well treated and Sekeletu, the chief's successor, continued to support them. During this time Livingstone and Oswell left the Chobe and saw the Zambezi for the first time. They indicated that the river was not previously known to exist in that area, as all the Portuguese maps put it further east.

After months of dust and parched plains, zebra enjoy the growth of lush grass that follow the rains. A blaze of colour from thousands of flowers heralds this season of renewal.

One of the great disappointments, though, was their discovery of a rampant trade in slaves with agents of the Portuguese, the Mambari. Many of the Makololo wore clothes of Western origin, even silk dressing gowns! Livingstone later learned that the Portuguese trader Silva Porto had been there already, in 1845. It was a bitter blow to Livingstone's dream of converting the people to Christianity. The wide rivers and the quantity of game, especially elephant, filled them with amazement. The Chobe is still a prime bastion of wildlife. An African river in all its primeval splendour, along which modern travellers can take leisurely boat trips and watch buffalo grazing on the banks or elephant swimming across the river. The evocative call of the fish eagle, with head thrown back, can be heard on every bend of the great river.

In November the rains came. During the late afternoon, thunder clouds turned the sky black behind the sunlit trees. At night, thunder rumbled closer and closer, eventually erupting in mighty crashes as lightning flashed across the night sky, silhouetting the trees in front of our tent. The rain fell, beating against the roof, making sleep impossible.

Within a day, the larger animals had vanished, released from their allegiance to the river. The elephants took advantage of the fresh green canopy that grew quickly in the mopane forests where there would now be rain-filled pans. The buffalo and zebra, too, had gone to the fresh grazing on some distant plain. Flowers covered the veld in a carpet of yellow and purple. Butterflies, moths and insects appeared in a season of new life, while termites took to the wing like a shower of confetti. The earth was damp and the dust had gone.

Frogs were everywhere, leaping around and croaking as they frantically sought a mate. Birds like the saddle-billed stork and the hammerkop found easy pickings amongst this seething mass.

Trying to drive around after heavy rains can be difficult. The roads are turned into rivers in places and you can expect to get stuck, especially on the muddy tracks across the flood-plains.

A week before, there had been great herds of elephant along the river, but now the campsite at Serondella was quiet. At night, though, the moths and

Zanjeelah, the boatman of the rapids.
T. Baines

insects were intolerable, attracted to any kind of light source, lantern or candle. One insect we had a great liking for was the dung beetle. I would like to quote the eloquent way in which Livingstone described it:

> The scavenger beetle is one of the most useful of insects, as it effectively answers the object indicated by the name . . . for no sooner are animal excretions dropped than, attracted by the scent, the scavengers are heard booming up the wind. They roll away the droppings of cattle at once, in round pieces often as large as billiard balls, and when they reach a place proper by its softness for the deposit of their eggs, and the safety of their young they dig the soil out from beneath the ball till they have quite let it down and covered it: they then lay their eggs within the mass. While the larvae are growing they devour the inside of the ball before coming above ground to begin the world for themselves. The beetles with their gigantic balls look like Atlas with the world on his back; only they go backwards and, with heads down, push with their hind legs. As we recommend the eland to John Bull, the gigantic frog to France [reference to the bull frog], we can confidently recommend this beetle to the dirty Italian towns and our own sanitary commissioners.

(Coleoptera scarabaeinae) Dung beetles shape dung into balls which are rolled away and buried as food for their larvae which hatch within the dung.

The rain is welcomed, not only by animals, but by people too. In this part of the world, where rains can be undependable, it is highly valued. 'Pula' means rain in Botswana and it is no coincidence that the country's currency also bears this name.

Crossing the border from Botswana into Zimbabwe can be a time-consuming business. However, once into Zimbabwe we were back on to tarred roads which took us swiftly through the Zambezi National Park towards Victoria Falls. The town is a bustling tourist centre with a number of hotels, the most imposing being the traditional colonial-styled Victoria Falls Hotel. The spray from the falls can be seen from the hotel gardens and it made me wonder what it must have been like to come here when it was a wilderness, 130 years ago. James Chapman gave a descriptive account of his first impressions in his diary on 23 July 1862:

> We halted for the night under a huge motsebe tree. When the frolicking of the little makalaka boys subsided we heard a murmuring and then a roaring like the dashing of a mighty surf on some rockbound coast . . . we had no idea of our distance from the falls but we knew we were near them. Next morning I walked about, hoping to fall in with game. On rounding the point of the high sandy ridge on which we had slept, my attention was directed to a glittering object through the trees. I ascended a tree with some difficulty and about six miles away beheld a line of smoking clouds, five large ones and many lesser, arising from a crack in the earth . . . thinking this first glimpse may escape [Thomas] Baines' eye, I made a rough sketch on two pages of my pocket book. . . . I left my perch, descended the sandy hill and crossed a rivulet flowing east . . . had not gone far before we saw a rhino . . . ascended another hill and had a view of the whole length of the falls and a gorge on our right . . . descended for twenty minutes from the hill through a forest until we stood upon the brink at one end. The first view broke upon us in its terrible grandeur and I could not help thinking what a discovery I lost in 1853.

Chapman and two friends had hired Makololo guides in the Chobe to take them by boat to the falls, but as they were about to set off they had news that Sekeletu and Livingstone had returned. The boatmen gave back their payments of beads and brass wire and refused to take the explorers. Chapman afterwards complained to Livingstone, who informed him that the Makololo were afraid of the Matabele, in whose territory the falls lay, and who had lately slaughtered a tribe for associating with the Makololo.

Chapman goes on, 'Had we known more than what was had from native reports we would have made a great effort to cut the Doctor out.' This was a strong implication that he suspected Livingstone was saving the falls for himself.

In his accounts of his attempts to photograph the falls, Chapman complained of 'all sorts of chemical difficulties'. Bear in mind the type of equipment he must have been using. Glass plate slides and a large bellows plate camera were a cumbersome and laborious way of doing photography, which was in its infancy. It was also necessary to develop the plate immediately after exposure, otherwise the image would fade.

The falls by Sunrise with the 'spray cloud' rising 1,200 feet.
T. Baines

Chapman continued, 'By a variety of mistakes I have been a fortnight without getting a picture while Baines is getting magnificent sketches.' Quite a different story today when photography is so instant.

Thomas Baines accompanied Chapman on most of his expeditions and was an exceptional artist, producing many candid impressions of Africa in the nineteenth century. Baines also accompanied Livingstone on the unsuccessful Zambezi expedition in 1858, but was one of many to displease the doctor, who sacked him on the dubious grounds of pilfering supplies for the Portuguese in Portuguese East Africa (Mozambique). However, history records Livingstone as the first European to reach the falls of Mosio a tunya, 'The Smoke that Thunders', in 1855. Livingstone's description of the falls was far more technical than Chapman's, though. He wrote:

> The Falls are singularly formed. They are simply the whole mass of the Zambezi waters rushing into a vent made right across the bed of the river. The river, flowing rapidly among numerous islands and from 800 to 1,000 yards wide meets the vent in its bed at least 100 feet deep and at right angles with its course, or nearly due east and west, leaps into it and becomes a boiling white mass at the bottom, ten or twelve yards wide.

Prompted later by his publisher in London, he added a more lyrical description: 'Scenes so lovely must have been gazed upon by angels in their flight.' Today you can take a flight from the nearby airfield to view the falls from the air, appropriately named 'The Flight of Angels'!

Giraffe emerge from the woodlands during the afternoon and can often be seen out on the floodplains at sunset.

Livingstone must have been impressed when he first viewed the falls, for he even inscribed his initials and the date on a tree on an island in the middle of the river. It should be noted that Livingstone had known of the existence of the falls for four years before he reached them, during which time he must have deemed other explorations to be more important. To be precise, his expedition to Luanda, in Portuguese Angola, in 1853, when he followed the Zambezi's course westward.

As he had already known of the falls, he would have considered them as a great obstacle to his 'navigable highway of God', meaning that any river traffic coming up the Zambezi from the east coast would have to terminate at the falls, impeding any direct access to the interior beyond.

Livingstone's journey to Luanda was nevertheless heroic and as he found himself on the west coast, his consequent journey back, via the Victoria Falls and then on to the mouth of the Zambezi in Portuguese East Africa (Mozambique), meant that he had crossed the African continent from coast to coast. This feat made him a living legend. The doctor had for some time been looking for some geographical feature to name after Queen Victoria and he considered the falls most suitable.

Approaching the falls today is far less of an adventure but nonetheless exciting. You can park at the entrance to the nature reserve and, having paid the entrance fees, you follow a clear pathway to Livingstone's statue which overlooks a magnificent view of the cascading water. One pathway descends quite far down the gorge and another leads through the rain-forest, which receives perpetual spray from the falls. This path takes you along the front of the falls on the opposite side of the gorge into which the Zambezi plunges some 100 metres. As you walk through the forest the sound is thunderous, as the gentle spray descends through the lush vegetation around you.

Bushbuck can sometimes be seen here. Imagine, though, what it must have been like when buffalo or rhino could be seen in front of the falls, with its ever-present rainbow framing the scene.

During the last 500,000 years the Zambezi has carved eight gorges and is in

A yellow-billed oxpecker (Buphagus africanus) can help in ridding a buffalo of parasites. This bird is a useful lookout, alerting its host to danger.

the process of constant change. The site of the present falls is not permanent. The Devil's Cataract is presently over 300 metres lower than the rest of the falls and is being deepened until eventually all the water will be able to escape down this channel in one rush. The cascades at the sides of the main falls will probably disappear, as the main body of water from the Zambezi will be channelled through the middle.

The Victoria Falls seemed a fitting end to our journey. We had discovered much about this part of Africa with its wealth of history. The hardships and danger, the discoveries, the elations and disappointments that these first explorers experienced in their solitary quests, caught the attention of the world and led to the colonization of Africa by European powers in the latter part of the nineteenth century. Whether the changes these nations brought to Africa were of benefit to its people is arguable, but they did bring about the end of the slave trade that Livingstone had so earnestly opposed.

Let us hope that these wonderful wild places can be preserved as Africa moves into the twenty-first century.

Breeding herds of hippos congregate on the floodplains. Each group occupies a stretch of the wide river, defended by a dominant bull.

The Chobe is a good place to watch elephants (Loxodonta africana) swimming. They cross over to the Caprivi Strip in Namibia where they graze overnight, returning to the sanctuary of the Chobe National Park the next morning.

The calves are boisterous and love to lark about in moments of relaxation out on the floodplain.

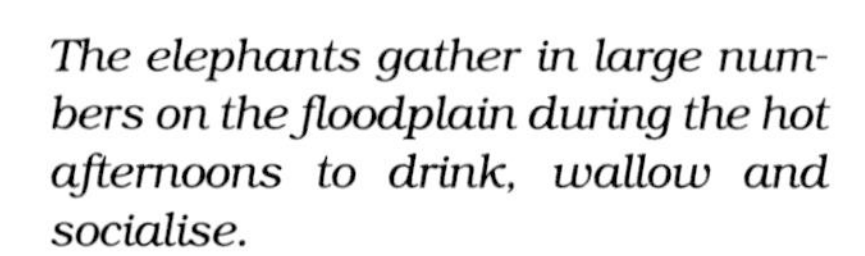

The elephants gather in large numbers on the floodplain during the hot afternoons to drink, wallow and socialise.

Like humans, elephant cows have two breasts on their chest. Calves enjoy the rich milk which contains bacteria, essential to the baby's immune system.

On the sandbanks the African skimmers (Rynchops flavirostris) claim their nest sites. The bird uses its lower mandible to scoop up small fish as it skims across the water.

OPPOSITE: *After the first rains, the carmine bee-eaters (Merops nubicus) use the steep banks for their nest sites, continually flying back with moths and other insects to feed their chicks.*

The floodplains attract many species of water-birds, like white pelicans (Pelicanus onocrotalus).

OPPOSITE: *In November the rains came. Black thunder clouds descended, creating a contrasting backdrop behind two egrets on their lofty perch.*

During the night the storm broke, lightning lit up the sky followed by a series of deafening crashes of thunder.

The pans soon filled with fresh rainwater, attracting many animals away from the rivers. Zebras on their way to the Mababe Depression stop at a rain-filled pan.

The rain is a cue for the elephants to disperse into the mopane forest, fresh with lush new growth. With so many pans holding water, they are seldom seen in large numbers during the summer months.

The tough mouth can chew the sharpest thorns and toughest bark.

Who said lions are boring? A young lion indulges in crazy antics as he finds out that he is now too big to climb small trees!

In a frantic orgy, mating frogs (Pixicephalus adspersus) leap around the shallow pools, but in their efforts to create new life they expose themselves to predators . . .

OPPOSITE: *. . . like this juvenile saddlebill stork . . .*

. . . or a hammerkop (scopus umbretta)

OPPOSITE: *Its legs covered in pollen, a blister beetle (Coleoptera meloidae) feeds on flowers. There are 350 species and all are poisonous.*

An impala keeps a close eye on her fawn. If a fawn loses its mother it is doomed for it would never be adopted. Each fawn has its own distinctive smell that the mother recognises.

OPPOSITE: *The yellow-billed stork (Ibis ibis) probes the river for hiding fish.*

Pythons (Python anchietal) lurk in the undergrowth, close to water.

Livingstone had been searching for a geographical feature to name after the queen. The falls of Mosio a tunya seemed most suitable.

The Zambezi plunges one hundred metres into the gorge.

The spray from the Falls creates a permanent rainbow.

BIBLIOGRAPHY

Chapman, J. *Travels in the Interior of Africa*, A.A. Balkema, Cape Town 1971.
Livingstone, D. *Missionary Travels in South Africa*, John Murray, London 1857.
Oswell, W.C. *William Cotton Oswell, Hunter and Explorer*, London 1900.
Roodt, V. *Trees of the Okavango Delta*, Shell Publications
Ross, K. *Jewel of the Kalahari*, BBC Publications
Wallis, J.P.R. *Thomas Baines*, A.A. Balkema, Cape Town 1976.

Elephants came regularly to bathe in front of camp on the Khwai River.

Photographs on pages 63, 144 and portrait of the author by Maggi Heinz.
Tree illustrations by Chris Harvey.